VIEWS FROM THE ISLAND
CHARLES E. WADSWORTH

*This
book is for
my wife Jeannie
my daughter Laurie
and my son Geoffrey
in the order in
which I came
to know
them.*

Yes, I confess I've always had a leaning
Toward poetry as the music of meaning.
I prefer such painting as preserves intact,
Means, meaning, mystery...miraculous in fact.

VIEWS FROM THE ISLAND

POETRY AND PRINTS
by
CHARLES E. WADSWORTH

THE TIDAL PRESS
1 9 7 8

WE HAVE ALL read that standard disclaimer found on one of the first few pages preceding a work of fiction which tends to run thus: "No character in this book is based on an actual person. If the reader encounters someone in these pages who seems to breathe and live that is a verbal illusion."—*which says something about the relative armament of libel laws compared to the disarming laws of art. Born out of a chance word, a passing incident or a casual anecdote, the island people you will meet in a number of the verses which follow are imagined composites. They are, however, as veritably downeast as I could make them. Those poems with dedications arose out of specific affection - and affection, I trust, is never a form of libel.*

Poems and Prints © Copyright by
Charles E. Wadsworth 1978
All Rights Reserved
Library of Congress No. 78-52619
ISBN—Trade No. 0-930954-05-X
      Deluxe   0-930954-05-8

THE TIDAL PRESS
Cranberry Isles, Maine 04625

TABLE OF CONTENTS

The Coast Of Maine

This is no sleepy land where lotus grows,
No place of indolence and languid doze
With dulcet winds and warm, seductive seas
To lull and woo you to a soft repose.
No plumage of palm fronds a silken strand.
Spear-head spruce, needle-sharp, secure a land
Whose sea-shocked cliffs neither yield nor appease.
Rock, here, has no plan ever to be sand.

Where islands sail seas clearer than reason,
Colder than justice, winds sharp as treason
Buffet stone-clad ships, dark-cargoed with trees
Through sobrieties of seas and season.

I've known places Edenic as a rose;
None knew so well the poetry of prose.

No Heavenly City

I've heard tell of a "heavenly city"
But I'll take my utopia rural;
Islanded in seas vaster than pity,
Evil seems less infinitely plural.
On this isle deadly sins aren't quite unknown,
(Where have they ever been or like to be?)
But with them some lively virtues — homegrown —
Flourish greenly as a seedling fir tree.

It's here a man has two co-equal rights,
The right to be neighborly if he would,
Or not to be, according to his lights;
And few to tell him how he shall or should.

I've noticed here I've often been used well,
Which is one way to tell heaven from hell.

The House

For Jeannie

We built it together, my wife and I;
A house of rock and wood upon a rock,
Just where the island's hard spine jutted high
Through a small field, about which woodlands flock.
To build a house should be no novelty;
To work a shape work and love can live in
Is as basic as anything can be,
An instinct as old as any given.

And yet it's true, when strangers passed that way
They seemed to think they'd found an island zoo
And paused to see the knowing creatures play,
Disbelieving the tricks they saw them do.

I never thought to hire nor did my wife,
Others to shape our house or build our life.

To An Island Lady

For Lena

It cannot be the same I know and yet...
Whenever I glance down the path between
Our house and hers, where now and then we met
And stopped to talk about the local scene —
Lobstering, the price of bread, life that stirred
Unsanctified, her reference as large
As she, marred by no pettiness of word,
With laughter most of all to clear and charge
The air with sanity—
                    I recollect
The times she bore the produce of her art,
Her kitchen lore. The trodden sods reflect
Her passing still; mute tracings of a heart
Addicted to the simple modes and rare.
The path is empty.
                    There is no one there.

4

Two Fishermen

For Harold

Facing a window on the sea, he weaves
The cunning nets, the glinting spindle deft,
Polished by twine and hours. An osprey cleaves
The air and sea, then cheated of his theft
And need arises and his scrutiny
Repeats. A web of frail feathers sustains
The cool stare and the cruel necessity.
Today he has drenched talons for his pains.

Smiling wryly, hand poised above the twine
The man says, "Missed!" and turns to his weaving.
"All that work and waiting and only brine
Between your toes. Well — you can't chew grieving!
Good chance brother; I'll spare you cod or hake,
Being both fish-hawks, some different in make."

John Donne And Islands

John Donne tells me and doubtless it's true,
"No man is an Island, intire of itself..."
There's much to be said for his point of view;
One book seems sterile alone on a shelf.
Today, unaccompanied, I strolled the beach;
Islands were strewn to the far horizon,
Each in its solitude, each within reach,
Each in the separate sea it plies on.

Fruit of the mainland, each has its savor,
Part of a family, yet quite unique;
Always that difference, some special flavor
Taunts you and teases, its onenesses pique.

Everything's seamless and all things sunder,
This is the burden, this is the wonder.

The Archipelago

The Coast and Geodetic charts attest
This is just one island quite separate,
Singular and distinct yet I'd suggest
That many isles make up the sum of it.

Panting refugees from towns and cities,
Most summer colonists romanticize
The island's beautiful severities.
Its beauty's harder won in native eyes,
Who, year-long, pay for that beauty the fee
Livelihoods exact. No one views it whole,
But through a lens of partiality,
Depending on the angle of each soul.

Though coastal surveys do not say it's so,
This island is an archipelago.

Equally Strange

Yesterday, strangely mesmerized by mist
The island seemed an unfamiliar place,
As though its own specter was keeping tryst
With it, less tryst though than unplanned embrace;
The shapes and place of spruce trees rearranged,
Reduced to floating tips rooted in fog,
The hyphenated boles of birch estranged
From earth, hard ledges steaming like a bog.

Today, infinite clarities of fact
Assault the eye in thronging precision
Until it seems to dim — a cataract
Of dazzling fact — obscuring my vision.

Transforming mist, transforming clarity,
Equally strange, mystify equally.

Chinese Maine

Obscurer than any philosophy,
The fog spins skeins around reality,
Dimming the sun where hills and fog debate
Intricate arguments of void and state.
Today is not quicksilver Taoist
To please a summer orientalist.
It's not to footnote any scholar's text
That the day's bewildered and the hills vexed
And blurred all out of focus by the fog,
But more in show that Nature's dialog,
Irresolute, mutable, roundabout,
Hesitates today between truth and doubt...
Except that she will not have them apart,
Holding them both to be the same at heart.

Fog

For Emily

All day the blindfold fog has gone in search,
About her now its caul of white is sewn,
It knows and claims her where she sits alone
On a coldly smoking log near the church
Whose planes dissolve among the buttress birch,
As though its matter were but soul on loan.
— An arm away her hands are not her own. —
One wet jay mentions blue skies from his perch.

Her world enfolds her, masks of mist thicken;
Within her hand a star-crowned tuft of moss,
As though repaying her for vision's loss
Burns in recompense, its green fires quicken.

This fog's bound to lift; new vistas wider
May bring her less than here where mists hide her.

The Shingle Beach

Through all the days and nights the gaming sea
In loss and gain, in tumbling roll and play
Hones rock on rock; in ceaseless lottery
Obeys the cold and lunar croupier.
The sovereign moon-man, alchemist of chance,
Drops grave and golden nets, the random bond
Of freedom and of fate where seas advance
Upon the shores and shores in turn respond.

Throb after throb, the waters fret and reach,
Leaving the wrack and wreckage there behind
Among the dicing pebbles on the beach,
Which click their chance caprice upon my mind.

Low tide, mean tide and ultimately flood,
Gaining and losing course the sea and blood.

Islands — Maine And Hellenic

Calymnos, Seriphos, Symi and Cos,
Mykonos, Santorin and Carpathos...
So ran my litany as a roamer,
Sun-stunned among sun-dumb isles of Homer.

Other names, plain-spoken yet romantic
Are scribed on the slate-blue North Atlantic:
Bear, Gott, Cranberry and Black — I see in
Them chronicles ancient as Aegean.
Their shrill tern calls are music I cherish,
Their cool, secret gods aren't like to perish.
Their seas, equally skilled as architect,
Hew columns in cliffs lucid pools reflect.

Granite temples, pinkly parthenonic,
Speak silence, eloquently laconic.

Deserted Islands

I've been told five thousand islands float
Off the coast of Maine, enough to satisfy
The isleophiles in every summer boat
Passing that way who cast a hungry eye
On each in turn and fall then to scheming
On which deserted one they'd make their own.
This they'd want: rocks; trees; a garden dreaming
Under bird song; a small, snug house bleached as bone.

But the deserted islands of August
Should not be put to January's test.
In far cities recall them if you must,
Floating in August oceans. That is best.

Recalling them dreaming. Be glad you aren't where
They endure — colder than dreams, lonely, bare.

The Mailboat

It's called the "mailboat" but I can't think why,
Considering the cargo on its decks.
Its superstructure jack-strawed on the sky
Looks like the random salvage from six wrecks:
Two refrigerators; tall timbers; ply-
Wood panels braced against the wind by checks
Of someone's groceries and sacks of dry
Cow dung; cheeping hen-chicks (guaranteed sex);
Fish-nets; bed-springs; someone's maul and grapples;
Up-turned bike-wheels, spokes splintering the light
Breeze, turning like some innovative sail;
A sapling hung with more hope than apples;
Posies for the school's graduation night —

And if my count be true — one sack of mail.

Fourth Class Post-Office
For Margie and Hilda

A mole-eyed bureaucrat brought it to pass
Somewhere in the blind catacombs of State;
A firm decision in sextuplicate:
Our postal category is Fourth Class.
But this post is more friendly than federal:
A foul weather shelter when you'd be warmed;
A place to be informed and misinformed;
To chat; to gossip; to be told and tell.

I think its class more First than Fourth. Not one
But two post-mistresses in turn dispense
Unofficial kindliness and a sense
That stamp-sales aren't the biggest business done,
Plus good-cheer no postal law provides for.

What First Class post-office could provide more?

Wild Pear

Forestry has dubbed wild pear "a weed tree",
Worthless in all the book-keeping of man,
But I'm not all that sure I would agree
When I weigh what it does in a year's span.

How could anyone bear Maine's coastal spring
— All dripping hours and promises deferred —
If it weren't for the wild pear's blossoming.
Its naked December grace, lightly furred
With snow-flake bloom, is memory on its mettle,
Pledging summer bloom, fruit where birds romp
Greedily and that first leaf turned petal -
Scarlet which signals autumn's dying pomp.

Some keep books with columns marked Store and Save,
Recording there what wild pear freely gave.

Angels In The Wild Pear

For Carl

A friend tells me, on one misty May dawn,
Just arisen and still in shrouds of sleep,
He glimpsed, where a curtain had not been drawn,
A sight which caused his laggard heart to leap.

Out in the meadow a wild pear that day
Bore the light burden of angelic flocks,
Their voices like far buoy bells at play,
Plaiting silver blooms through their golden locks.

I tell it as he told me the story:
It may be they were only gulls at rest,
Tranced by sleep into a morning glory,
Their wings and wails mistaken for the blest.

Still — God help us all if we never see
At least one angel in a wild pear tree.

A Wild Pear In East Dean

For Christopher

Linnaeus himself would have approved of
Christopher's guided garden tour as he
Named for us each specimen tenderly,
Mixing precisely botany and love.
"That," he said, gesturing with his pipe-stem
Toward a sapling which rose near a half-seen
Sculptured boy, half-patined with England's green,
"Is an amelanchier. I'm fond of them."

Amelanchier to me — if not botany —
Is wild pear. The word whisked me away
To frothing tides of wild pear bloom in May,
Flooding dark groves with luminosity.

On his isle he'd see amelanchier blow,
But never the wild pear spate Maine isles know.

The Beachcombers

For Laurie

You were so young then, four or five, no more.
We walked amid the sea's recurring speech
And watched its old embroilment with the shore,
Culling small tidal treasures from the beach:
Sleek stones, sanded glass, shells and once a toy,
A wooden horse lost overboard, as ears
Cupped the plaints of another girl or boy
And fondled smooth by oceanic tears.

Now you're a woman grown or near, your eyes
Are expectant of a larger treasure.
The shore you walk and search will yield surprise,
But, oh my child, how different the measure.

Time will bring song and gifts; time will entice.
Time will bring loveliness; time will bring price.

In Praise Of Critics

Around us fades the day and plaintive themes,
Bach and Handel's kinder simplicities,
Fashioned by them in artful, artless schemes
For those surer of love than masteries;
Our audience, no glib aesthetes, so free
With carping and so niggardly with praise,
But measures of meadow, cleft rocks and sea,
In tune with our recorder's rustic ways.

And now it's dusk. We cannot read the notes
And hear, introduced with softest reserve,
Then swelling from two Mozart, robin throats
Fluencies of grace we do not deserve.

Woodwind practitioners, practiced as time,
As critics and lovers they're lightly sublime.

Fire-Ties

Behind us dim the last, light, twilit notes
Recorders strewed in summer airs and shakes;
Within a hush and gleam the rowboat floats,
Whiter than phosphorescent triple wakes.
A keel line's drawn upon the quaking fire
From cold whirlpools the dipping oars incite,
Flickering cones which flare and then expire;
Liquid galaxies, oar-tips re-ignite.

One star falls as we near the rose-held banks
Through the perfumed patterns of the fire-flies.
The diminished milky-way of their ranks,
Mirroring the sky's, is doubled fire-ties.

This night, earth, sea and sky are in fire-bloom;
Three gifts of darkness, darkness can't consume.

The Defender

He explained it all to me carefully:
The impulse toward bird-song; the way they live;
All about territoriality...
Song was a challenge. (It was persuasive,
His explanation.) Song was really threat
And boast, possession the theme — and refrain.
Other cocks hearing that lyric gauntlet
Flung through air would retreat from that domain.

Yet this morning, one that you'd remember,
Round as a tenor, perched high on our fence,
A robin with a breast like an ember
Sang ceaselessly in not quite defiance.

It seemed he was singing for nothing less
Than song or more — and as perfectly useless.

The Piper-Prince

For Ashley

Africa's suns burn skies away from Maine
And yet today I swear I saw its prince,
Wearing regalities that made me wince
In wonder that our isle could entertain
Such a sojourner. Flagrant royal, in dress
Of purples, pink and puce, he trod the road
In careless splendor as though his abode
Was any land his footsteps chanced to press.

From a pouch woven of some peacock stuff
He plucked a pipe from out its secret hoard,
Paused, laughed and sweetening his leisure, poured
Forth wild, free tunes that made a sailboat luff,
And stunned all the birds in admiration —
Except one — who sang in emulation.

Sand Peeps

For Tud

I've met none who told a story better,
He knew just when and how to nudge a fact,
When to hew the line and keep the letter
And when to fabricate with verve and tact.
He needed no literary caucus
To tell him which or how or what to say;
Knowing what the point of all good talk is
He had the knack to make words work or play.

When he rubbed fact on the flesh of fiction
The children he called "sand peeps" sat enrapt,
Their eyes big with the sparks of that friction,
Captive to his yarns and glad to be trapped.

Best judges of the game called "Let's Pretend",
The children heard him out from end to end.

The Smallest Island

This is the smallest island in the sea,
Or at least I've yet to see one smaller:
One tip of ledge; some gravel and a tree.
On the mainland younger trees grow taller,
Though theirs is not a lush economy.
Here, upon the spare and barren islet
A stage is set with one live property.
Heired and shaped by gales and icy quiet,
Sparely branched where wasting tides fall and rise,
Pruned by the blown salt of marine riot,
It turns its hunger, the granite diet,
Into votive greens for spring and defies
Congealing tides. It lights three taper cones.
Brave incontinence fuels its wintry bones.

Two Brothers — Jeremiah
Keeping Faith

Unexpected luck, good fortune that warms
Elicited from him no hosanna;
Balmy zephyrs reminded him of storms,
His forecasts were mammon more than manna.
In regard to endless loaves and fishes,
He shook his head and he muttered sadly.
Miracles like that he held were vicious,
Depressing the market's prices badly.

So — when old Jeremiah left this strife
The parson and his neighbors were aghast,
Solemnly mindful that in Jare's new life
He'd have nothing to complain of at last.

But rumor reached them that he, safely there,
Looking down, found heaven could not compare.

Two Brothers — Jedidiah

The Fall From Grace

Frolic was less his mode than disaster;
He wasn't out to be hope's easy dupe.
Bound to strangle us fast, if not faster,
He saw the round world as a hangman's loop.
As a sour seer he collected doom,
Yet the old men yarning and making myth
Seemed to need his fidelity to gloom,
Their tales shining by comparison with.

Then one day I missed him from the landing;
Somehow the fore-noon air had lost its salt.
"Where's Jedidiah?" I asked. One standing
By brought his squealing tackle to a halt.

"Gone to hospital. Went and made a joke.
First time for that — when he smiled something broke."

Feather And Pebble

Whatever else she is — Nature is change;
That is her prime and primary passion.
Nothing's done but she must then rearrange
Whatever she's just chosen to fashion.
All that we label and identify
Disappear yet disappearing insist
They're as permanent as the drifting sky,
Whose shifting flux is a way to persist.

A feather, light as its own reflection
Is water-borne on air turned filaments.
That drowned pebble may be on inspection,
A mountain worn impenetrably dense.

And one day, though who knows when or whether,
Feather may be stone and stone be feather.

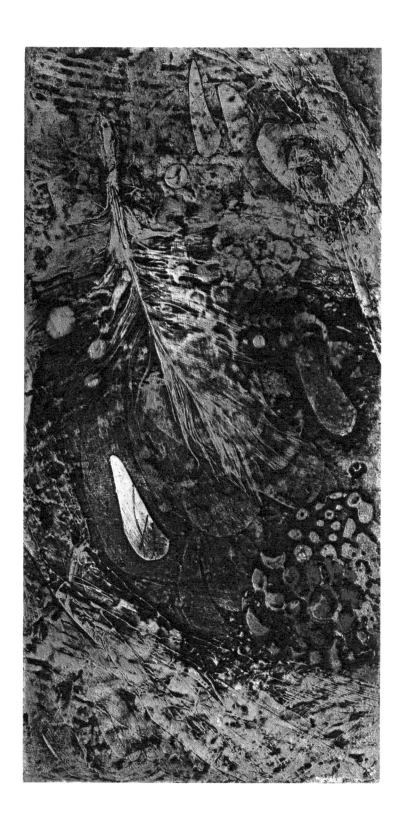

Tidal Pool

I've seen no tidal pool that held much less:
One red pebble, burnished by stringency;
A seedling lobster's pink transparency,
So subtle as almost not to be there;
A trace of seaweed, finely spun and spare,
Torn perhaps from a drowning mermaid's head;
A few bright stains, as though the stones had bled;
Spoke wordlessly of things I could not guess.

Time and tides hung suspended in the pool,
Though a ripple of a ripple falling
Across its face, said, the sea, recalling
This strayed small cup and portion of itself,
Planned soon to re-submerge the granite shelf
And so regain its lost and cryptic jewel.

A Braider Of Rugs

For Pink

The ladies of the island would concede
Hers were the tightest, the best rugs braided,
Stout as the houses generations deed,
Crafted to withstand time's feet unaided.

But more than craft was bound into her rugs —
Seeing what seeing eyes she brought to bear
On distance and the smallest plant that hugs
A ledge. She missed nothing, always aware
Of the live source and substance of her art.
Yet she would never think to call it that,
Feeling it a fancy word, set apart
From the dailiness of all she worked at.

Though I've been told, art is mind heart and hand,
Intimate in one vivid, braided strand.

Caning Chairs

He'd shipped on almost everything that floats;
Now he caned torn chairs on his front door stoop,
Warped fingers pulling taut each pliant loop,
Where he could watch the traffic of the boats.
The tangled script of wrinkles on his face,
More intricate and mazed than cross-rip seas,
As though unsnarling time's perplexities,
He translated into the cane's strait lace.

Stopping by one day I heard him declare,
"I've known it easy some but most times tough;
Troubles in good supply; one life's enough.
Forevermore could get to be a care.
Still...
      all in all...
            reckoning carefully...
Life's the best thing ever happened to me."

The Oar

As masters go the sea's cruel as any;
Yes, he'd known it, its every trick and mood,
Drawing from it every salt-caked penny.
Sweat was the sauce that flavored all his food.

Once he told me, oar upon his shoulder,
"I'll just lug this oar to — I don't know where,
Till I can't hear a sea-battered boulder,
Till someone says, 'What's that your totin there?'
That's the place, the spot I'm bound to settle,
I'll plant my oar like an unlit light-house,
I'll work just enough to keep in fettle,
I'll build me, past sea-sounds, a small, tight house."

He shrugged. "But a man could get too much slack.
I'd hear the sea nights. I'd soon be bound back."

Gull Flight

No breed I know has quite that high disdain,
None utilizes emptiness so well,
Revealing where the unseen contours swell,
The densities of space made freely plain,
Their couse in wheeling, lifting, falling flight
A matter of the slightest shift and stir;
Feathers, pressed above, held below, quiver
In the substantial currents of the light.

You might think, if no one told you better,
Seeing their casual routes, their easy haste,
They led lives of untethered, white and chaste
Indifference to every bond and fetter —

Except one scream and plunge with famished glee,
Slipping down the sound to the waiting sea.

The Wary Crow

Everything which begins must have an end.
Although I do not like to think it's so,
Someday I expect someone I don't know
Will land upon this island and will wend
His way over paths and trails which now bend
Through the forest and fields so men can go
Easily from house to house, to and fro,
On affairs of love and hate, take and lend;

Finding the roads all reduced to traces,
The paths grown greener, nearly lost to sight
And spy above, a flock of crows in flight
And peer through lilac screens for lost faces
And wonder what had been the fatal flaw
And hear one shrewd, wise, wary black crow caw.

The Dead Crow

What sly and unforeseen foe brought him low,
Crumpling him on this snow-streaked, bitter beach?
Few living things are crafty as a crow;
To snatch him death would need a long, sure reach.

Shrewd swaggerer, who seldom missed a thing,
Raucous roisterer, this black buccaneer,
Who'd spent his days in brazen plundering,
With sure cock-sure competence — need he fear?

The keenest sentry, from his haughty perch
He oversaw the flock's weal and wrangles.
Now, hoisted by cold, curled claws, his wings lurch
Like broken shadows — the blind head dangles.

That dark buccaneer, who boards silently,
He failed to see —

        as we won't —

           finally.

The Hummingbird

There's always something better than the best:

I thought today, watching the chickadees
Dodge through latticed larch twigs with flippant ease,
Or ride the breeze like seeds in comic zest
And sport, tumbling to upside-down arrest
Like some sure clowns upon the high trapeze;
There's nothing feathered flies so deft as these
Or lands to such a pert and vibrant rest.

And then I saw upon astonished air,
A trifle move with even surer grace,
Wantoning with gravity as in jest,
On blurred wings, more butterfly bright and fair
Than the flowers it hummed to, face by face.

There's always something better than the best.

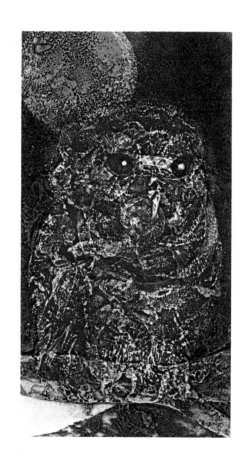

The Owlet

The mother owl and brood tonight like flakes
Of ash slow-spilling from a moon-singed sky
Drifted past with the sound "nothing" makes.

They were there and then gone before my eye
Could register their felted hunter's flight,
Quietly as the echo of a sigh —

Though I seemed to see by some tic of sight
One scrap veer away from the family prowl
And land on a shadowed branch to my right.

Slowly I wheeled my light; an atom owl
Suddenly was there, in nimbused surprise,
Banked moons burning below the cloud-soft cowl.

Ember-eyed bird — fledgling-new, antique-wise —
None so young wrests from night two moons for eyes.

The Heron Cove

Sculling slowly through the early morning
We were startled to see a heron rise
Above the sheer rock-face, without warning,
Swimming with gawky grace through liquid skies.

A gap breaching the forbidding borders,
We slipped through into listening silence,
Heron haunted, unused to marauders,
So reflective and still oars did violence
To sky-echoing waters and hovered
Where the surface and the bottom seemed betwixt,
On tree boughs with leaves and singing fishes mixed.

Bewitched, we seemed part swimming in the air,
Part breathing under spellbound waters there.

Survivors

Deliberately, he scrapes and smooths and sands,
Not quite obliterating all the years
Have scored upon the dinghy and his hands,
Crooked to his trade, his special tools and gears.

Varnish strokes, leveling to honeyed glass
In which the grain of wood and face fuses,
Reflect doubly all that has come to pass
Of stains and scars, blemishes and bruises.

Fifty years of tides, storms and shortened scopes,
The submerged ambush of gutting ledges
And shoals conspiring against youth and hopes
Acquaint you with all disaster's edges.

Nothing's so unglamourous as duty;
How curious this residue — beauty.

The Ship-Wright

They don't build men quite like him any more;
A man who'd been shaped by his shaping tools,
With no decked out fripperies aft or fore
In speech or dress. He left that to the fools
Who were taken in by, who set much store
By gimcrack pleasure craft. He lived by rules
The sea's laid down since men along its shore
Had mustered up courage for the long duels
Between them and it for a harsh living.
His boats had been designed by blow and gale,
And he himself seemed an adzed slab of oak.

He knew the price of a scanted giving,
And the final cost if his boats should fail.
He spoke little.
                        Men listened when he spoke.

A Thing Or Two

With smart movements, not one motion wasted,
She plucked the swaying laundry from the line,
Folding each clean ghost from where she'd placed it.
"There," she said, and paused a bit, "I'd opine
There's a right way and a wrong way to do
Anything." And then chuckled to herself.
"Though oldsters like me know the thing or two
They've learned may be all that's left on the shelf
Of what they used to know."

                    Just then a sheet,
Snatched by a grappling gust, wrapped her from knees
To nose like grave sculpture still in its veil.

"There's two truths I'll take to the judgement seat,"
She said, muffled. "Don't fold sheets toward a breeze,
Or worse yet, toss slop-water toward a gale."

The Lichened Ledge

Thrust seaward, a clenched fist of lichened ledge
Has long quarreled with abrading spray and gale;
Adamant as violence it will prevail,
Though sea-forces would blunt its flinty edge.
Proof too against insinuating seed,
Its nearly fissureless surface denies
Them cracks and chinks to colonize;
Though one invasion of vegetable need
Has managed a lichen establishment,
Its whorled, mottled flames a clinging gold.
Not quite plant and not quite not, its toehold
Tapestry hints one day ledge may relent,
That its almost timeless adamancy
Was molten stuff once and again might be.

The Lighthouse

"Down the shore there, before the lighthouse came,
I've lit a Judas-light or two," he said.
"Never knew the vessel's or the crew's name,
Or cared; don't pay to weep over the dead."
I have heard of a widespread sin called Greed,
And met those who boast of their addiction
To it, who'd not be caught dead with one good deed
Marring pure sin. His tale seemed purer fiction.

Though if true, if he never spoke *Neighbor,*
—A difficult tongue, confused in grammar —
The lighthouse speaks it now with small labor,
Speaks it lightly, with small hitch or stammer.

As hard a language as will ever be,
It speaks it brightly — almost perfectly.

Friends

Eb took a drink or two, then three or four
Or five or six or even seven too,
Until drinking was all that he could do,
That and a walk now and then to the shore.

His boat rotted and his wife left his bed;
His taxes unpaid, the town took his house
And Eb's role was fixed as the town's sad souse.
There wasn't much behind and less ahead.

He had one friend only as things waxed worse,
A one-eyed tomcat, peevish and morose.
Lonely and rejected, these two stuck close,
As close as sorrow round the old town hearse.

Eb, like Satan, wept at the tomcat's end,
Not for lack of heaven but lack of friend.

The Instructed Eulogy

Bertram's passing was met with composure,
The island managed to contain its grief,
His habit having long been foreclosure
This last one seemed at most a great relief.

Only those whose charity was reckless
Could spin from Bert's past some brief tales glowing
With feeble luster; few men so feckless
Had left their fellows with so much owing.

Yet even the death of a ne'er-do-well
Is death; that knowledge bode in each one's eyes.
If just the spotless rate a fare-thee-well
Parsons would never get to eulogize.

Ours was warned, lest he be carried away,
"Bert aint too much improved since yesterday."

The Kite

For Geoff

This is the proper season for a kite;
This is the proper month to set a sail.
Although today the wind's too strong a mite
The two of us will wander to the shore,
Treading torn breezes to the forest floor.
"It will fly," he'll say, his boy's eyes gleaming.
"It will crack the sky, sail right through and more."

"Perhaps it will," I'll think, "till heaven's gates
Are obstacles, and when a song relates
The incident, cherubim choirs will tell
How the bright message beat against the grates
In wind-strummed melodies that kite cords sing
And how a boy's heart climbed a living string,
Higher than high, higher than anything."

On The Death Of A Young Dog Named Moses

I don't know why the boy named him Moses,
More fisherman pup than social critic.
Certainly none who'd known him supposes
Ancestrys prophetic or semitic;
Unless, in some saints and seers there is much
Of a talent for love and innocence.
To anyone who had some use for such
Bounties, he had them lavish to dispense.

Young for malice, too unschooled to be mean,
Eyes in the raccoon, panda face alight
He went to meet the juggernaut machine;
His scream was knowledge, his wisdom fright.

No Moses, he'd have picked the world at hand,
Wicked, lovely, unexplored — promised land.

The Rescue

An old account tells of a drowning boy,
Out of breath, out of depth and out of hope,
Who suddenly was on the living slope
Of a form supple as the shape of joy.
Faster than the waves could follow after,
He was carried to refuge on the land;
Thinking back he could never understand
Why the air then trembled with soft laughter.

Was it some notion that the boy was kin
That moved the warm-blooded heart to the deed,
Or feelings older than family or creed,
Of wider, simpler, deeper origin?

When sea, sky and I vie for deepest grey,
To see dolphins leap saves a drowning day.

My War Of The Roses

Yes, I have fought my war of the roses
And I am willing to concede defeat.
Someday, where now the garden grows in neat
And ordered rows, wild roses will return.
The plot was theirs once and none proposes
Lettuce, beans, peas or corn will supplant them.
Root and rout them out, shovel dig and burn —
Yet they will persist. No need to plant them
If you'd make them a crop. One nub of root
Is all it takes to bring them surging back;
The first ground-sprung sprig, poised for swift attack
Is legioned stems, blossoms and ruddy fruit.

Beauty, they urge, survives insults and scorns,
If rooted in earth and if it has thorns.

The Parson's Gardens

For Doctor C.

Eternal life's a parson's stock in trade
And heaven the haven he seeks, though he,
Working his garden patch with hoe and spade,
Seemed just as much homely as heavenly.
Bending above the tender seedlings there
Or in the pulpit Sundays weeding sin
From our souls, separating wheat from tare,
He seemed to both gardens equally kin.

Bent closer to earth each spring, finally prone,
He confirmed, at last, that wheat and tares were one,
That heaven and the earth could not alone
Exist, that all ends where all had begun.

His road to heaven was no more high than low,
On his going he had not far to go.

Digging Potatoes

For Leslie

The blossoms withered, the haulms drooping low,
We dug in sea-weed loam with probing tines,
Both tyros as far as potatoes go.
One whose crop was words; one shapes, colors, lines,
We uncovered, as nubbled nuggets rose
To light, excitement older, as intense
As any, any art could yield to those
Who till the intangible fields of sense;
And probed as gently and as carefully
Amid the compost of each other's days,
Not knowing how large either crop would be
Or just what would surface to meet our gaze.

The harvest gathered there could have been worse
Than new potatoes, friendship and this verse.

Sweet Corn

A small subject for sonnet or psalter,
A minor matter, a plebian theme,
Yet this sight can make my pulses falter —
Indented ingots in an incensed steam,
Sweetly tabled on a pine-plank altar.

No Mayan or Incan, I sing its praise
As did they, who forecast in figured gold
The length of their temple's and their own days,
But trusted most auguries which foretold
Their future in the living gold of maize.

I hold my garden's mean without sweet-corn;
Nourishing it may be but not tonic,
Like a moral victory somehow forlorn
Or a marriage that's glumly platonic.

Blue-Berries

Although they're called "blue-berries" it *is* true,
Picking them slowly, cluster by cluster,
Noting their powdery, purplish luster
And juice like purple ink, purple's more their hue.
Yet purple's a shade too royal for their caste.
Low-borne, tough, tenacious, they will thrive
Where more regal high-born stock won't survive.
From little soil or less, roots clinging fast
In acid earth, they patiently condense
Out of summer days, the infinite hues
Of island seas and skies; their hoarded blues
Yielding a rare, common, honeyed essence.

"Blue" is this berry's simple aim and name,
Skies make no higher — seas no deeper claim.

Three Forests

Glancing up from a woods-path known to me
I thought, these trees are scrub in girth and reach
Compared to sequoias, live-oaks and beech,
Yet their reticent grandeur will do me.
And knew, glancing down at ground-cover where
Minuter forests of assorted moss,
Lichen and fungi grew, no sense of loss
Frets unseen inhabitants who live there.

Fir, birch and spruce is all the majesty
I need, as smaller creatures at my feet
Settle gladly for forests as complete
To them as my taller trees are to me;

As God may find peace beneath branching light,
Though something may glance down from higher height.

Both Skies

The lupine leaves in breathless symmetry
Enclose a drop of water where they meet
To make a scalloped cup atop the neat
And shining stem, an arc of purity.

Everything's held in that first morning hush;
Why even the birds give no song or sign!
The shore-bound sea, torpid in a feline
Sleep, has suspended the surf's hissing rush.

I see distilled in the clear drop of dew
Space bated to an essence hard to feel,
A sky so distant-small I almost reel;
Twice infinity, boundlessness times two.

Suddenly one gull wings through both in proof
Twice-timed blue can be habitation's roof.

Some Lesser Poets

For Jack

Dinner done we lolled about the table,
Stuffed with chowder and the virtues of work
Having painted the best we were able
All that day, having earned the right to shirk.

Someone said without preface or quibbling,
"Let's write a poem." One art down, one to go...
And without ado we set to scribbling
Unimpeded by crafts we did not know.

We stubbed our toes on towering attitudes,
Glib pens soon stuttered on the rocks of choice
And great thoughts dwindled into platitudes
Stumbling through thickets of a foreign voice.

But one sat still, owlish wise, Buddha mild,
Then wrote, "Oh, I am a clam...Damn..." and smiled.

The Sweet Centenarian

She answered the prim questions, one by one,
"How does it feel to be a hundred years?"
"Just twice as bad as fifty it appears."
She blinked and hitched her chair into the sun,
"Though I reckon now I've the hang of it
I'll go on; life's a habit hard to shake,
Anyway, I'm not one to bellyache."
The young man started at the tang of it.
—Decorum is expected of the old —
Noting it she felt that she'd been chidden.
"You're spry. Have you ever been bed-ridden?"
She nodded sweetly but her eyes were bold,

"Oh, yes," she said, warming to her story,
"Many times and thrice within a dory."

The Minor Gift

Toil was never the thing Seth most enjoyed,
None he had ever met was quite his style,
Being more apt to callous than beguile,
Consequently he was self unemployed.
He felt his talents were executive,
Those you might find in the best over-seer,
So most of his time was spent on the pier
Advising others how to work and live.

Dispensing dubious chapter and verse
Seth sometimes felt the edge of short, sharp shrift.
The replies were often less than terse,
Yet the toughest chores did give Seth a lift.

His presence lent sinews to each man's curse
And this is a true — if a minor gift.

Contra-Dance

I recall him at every school-house dance,
His youth a warmth of halo on the air;
Although judging from one young lady's glance,
Saintliness wasn't what she most saw there.

And he in turn was not quite unaware
Of the figure which he cut, when by chance
Their hands would meet and make of four a pair
In the fleeting encounters of the dance.

His first boat finished on a day of snow,
Nothing would do, he must then take her out...
"Snow's worse than fog," they warned, but he *would* go,
Sure that youth could put any storm to rout.

They found him — frozen — on a nearby beach,
Hands out-stretched for a partner out of reach.

The Cellar-Hole

Beneath a rough-quilled circle of the sky,
Which opened in the dense bough-roof of spruce,
Affirming man or men had once passed by,
We stumbled on a cellar-hole of loose,
Fallen stone, home now to wild rose and hare,
With a few adzed, mortised beams, gone to dote,
Wasted as hands which had hewn them with care,
And off to one corner the warmest note —
A stove, rust-red as the lichens creeping
On littered rocks it canted on askew,
Dark within, no spruce-fed, flame-heart leaping
Toward the seduction of the sky-drawn flue,
Slowly, slowly burning from shape to air,
Burning again the dreams once kindled there.

The Hurricane's Passage

It's calm, the hurricane has had its way,
Leaving behind shriven air and the mute
Disorder of its wake, a god in play,
Strewing trees, shredding leaf and branch and root,
Preferring beach rocks set in forest moss,
Seashells blooming on the grass like flowers,
Buoys stranded on earth's slow pitch and toss
And lobster-traps to catch summer showers.

No antic god engaged in gentle whim
Leaves all this shivered evidence of rage;
The roiled waters, torn to the eye's far rim
Remember violences I cannot gauge.

Fourteen fine lines cast no snare upon it,
Fiercer than verse, wilder than a sonnet.

After The Picnic

Here, where flagging day's one shrill sound is gulls
Extorting picnic hand-outs on the rocks,
Above where the summer sea steeps and mulls
In lazy discontent and muted shocks,
We absorb lobsters, the tint of sunset,
The sweet corn and the hint of haze that blurs
And flattens to a fishing silhouette,
The children. The flickering fire murmurs;
Littered about it, fallen flakes of flame
Among the orange lichen, glow the shards
Of lobster shells. The dachshund sleeps. The same
Old, enduring island-ledge girds and guards.

From mist-born isles afloat, a siren croon
Drifts to where we float on the afternoon.

Bacchus Basks On The Hearth

For Bacchus

Compactly curved as an Eskimo seal
Carved in soapstone, polished by fire-gleam,
Curled and content, the basking dachshund sleeps.
Then abruptly quakes as quick shudders steal
Across the toasted pelt, while deep in dream,
Eyelids twitch, lips peel, his heart thumps and leaps.

What grand revisions of his average day
Sleep brings I don't know: perhaps the chance fawn
He'd flushed while bumbling on a blunder-walk
Becomes the rout of twelve-pronged bucks at bay;
That humbling flight from a tom-cat's clawed brawn
Sleep transforms to triumphant tiger-stalk...

As we, in dreams, feeling no pangs or pains,
At times, too, may imagine we're Great Danes.

Winter Kitchen — 1

You rise fumbling, reluctant to awake;
Shiver stove-ward through night's stored up winter,
Hoping the black ice-cube will not splinter
To sharp fragments when you give it a shake.
On some mornings porous petals of frost
Climb the panes like June daisies redesigned
In a medium colder, more refined,
Suggesting summer'd been mislaid, not lost.

More real than memory the frost-flowers glow
With snow-field light; blooms that won't winter-kill
They shrivel when I set the stove afire.
Like visions too brittle for desire,
They flee to white meadows and, winter-still,
Wait June's daisy storm of warm, ragged snow.

Winter Kitchen — 2

A kitchen stove, shafting the floor with light
From a nicely set draft is what a man
Needs most when scything sleet-knives shred the night
Outside and would him too, much sooner than
He thinks if he were out. Then, to hitch in
Close to the stove's purring conversation
As it revives summer in the kitchen
Is warm as he'll be — short of cremation.

Though he needs too, dry stove-wood stacked in tiers,
Piled high, like scrolls from ancient libraries
Chronicling, ring by ring, dead summer years,
Re-lived now in murmuring reveries.

A twice-told tale, in leaves of flame unrolled,
Summers die again when the stove grows cold.

Clearing A View

Winter is best, though rainy days will do;
Winter's best for burning; fire cannot run
Upon the snow. The task is never done
Of unveiling far islands for the view
Of hills embossed on blues where light glances
Off spindrift tides and rides the backs of birds,
Or softly, lowly like barely heard words
Fogs nuzzle in with swaddling advances.

We fell and clear and burn, the trimmings fed
To flames and smoke; eddied pillars fusing
Rise from the clearing where we work, musing
On May vistas with Christmas hardly fled.

Trees we treasure topple when gale winds spin;
Those in our view last, rooted deep as sin.

Burning Brush

The sea's in hibernation now, it breathes
Lowly and scarcely paws the surly beach.
The sky is barred with grey and bleakly seethes
With snow. The mountains fade and bleach.
Only the fire warms where we attend,
Stoking it with underbrush, with alder
Festooned with catkins and tight buds which bend
Branches cranky on the flames — then falter.

Their buds, deceived by ill-timed warmth and sheen
Unclench, victims of a passing fashion,
Their guardian sheathes fan in a fledgling preen;
Then writhe and crisp, callow greens go ashen.

When winter's slow, cold fingers curl and cling,
Unwrap them gently — within them is Spring.

The Bright Burden

Last night first skirted freeze, then skirted thaw,
Tight-roping thirty-two degrees. Tip-toe
Rain fell softly — not quite rain, not quite snow —
Glazing every birch with ice till I saw
Next morning when I woke the splintered sun-
Rays glittering on branch and stem in drifts
Of stars night no longer needed, now gifts
Too generous to bear. Fewer would have done,
Since for such dual brilliance a price is paid
That even birches which best give and bend
Find high. Too starred, their giving grace may rend
And break, by too bright burdens over-weighed.

They too can be torn, toppled and riven
By more than they need or should be given.

Decoration Day

This is the day when all the graves are bright
With bouquets and small, brave flags sprung from grass
Freshly trimmed and fragrant from the dews night
Spread, still sparkling like drops of pure, green glass.

The grave of Gid's wife won't be neglected,
Though it's said, when she lived, as often foes
As friends, they fought more than is expected
By those who know how union often goes.
"Git me a wreath," he'd said. "Not a real one.
Them plastic ones can outlast storm and fuss.
Here's two dollars so you won't go steal one."
We'd discharged for Gid the charge he gave us.

Squabbling and love, he'd known, can walk together,
Immune as fake blooms to each other's weather.

Uncharted

A cove uncelebrated and apart,
Its mouth fraught with fanged rock and frothing spray,
It had no designation on the chart,
As though visitors had been warned away.
We approaching it then had small desire
To test the rumors of its being there
Yet coming far felt we should not retire,
So set a course for its mouth, true and fair.

And holding breath, slipped through the churning spume
To find ourselves in stillness so intense
It rang with quiet like an empty room
Which seems too small for something too immense.

This may be how our every voyage trends,
From disquiet through hazard to still ends.

Island Graveyard

Stiller than sudden silences they sleep.
It wasn't their turning tilted head-stones
Strewn through birches whiter than their dead bones
Which dapple grasses no one cares to reap.
Faintly the shore-spun rote, in measured play
Filters through the turf; every leaf-tongued tree
Speaks to them; they cannot reply, those clay-
Dumb members of the great majority.

A few rails remain of the crumbling fence
Confining those quietest of tenants —
They won't mind if I should steal some pennants
Of wild flag; memorials here grown dense.

They won't miss them or me. Home I'm needed.
Hearth wood's to be split, a garden weeded.

SOME AFTERVIEWS

IF YOU HAVE spent thirty-five years of your life practicing an art and the better part of each year for thirty years on a Maine island, you're bound to have thought some about both. You would like more spacious confines than are allowed by verse for a leisurely examination of those thoughts. Not to ferret out an air-tight theory of art and life (both begin where theory leaves off), but to see whether you have come upon any insights and inklings worth preserving. In much the same way, you walk a stony beach and spy a few pebbles so simple and so complete yet so allusive in form and design you cannot pass them by.

So far as I know, the only way you can be native to a place is to be born there. I plead a nativity of the heart. My attempt has been to see one island through the twin lenses of wonder and delight. I have made an act of praise using the dual mediums of prints and verse. Neither delight nor wonder is currently fashionable in the arts. But it takes a svelter figure than mine to turn the intellectual somersaults required if one wants to keep up with every new style in eternal truth.

The flavor of these pages is by choice insular and personal since everything universal is also insular, and since I have never met a people who was not a person. The skilled astronomer can move confidently from midnight star to midnight star. That same astronomer might run into some trouble steering from one Maine island to another through the soft deceits of a summer fog. To have been a painter most of your life isn't necessarily the best preparation for writing poetry. On the other hand, there is some difference of opinion about the best apprenticeship for either trade. To speak your mother tongue for sixty years should give you a speaking acquaintance with it. To decide not only that you will write verse but will write sonnets is a compound presumption. The novice is warned against the form. In an age that equates innovation with value, the canons of the sonnet are held to be proof of its exhaustion. But forms are never really exhausted, only those who practice them. It is just as likely that the avid quest for novelty is a sign of weariness. Any convention can be formal and empty. Innovations (the new formalities) can also be empty. Both, if hollow, make a remarkably similar sound when life bumps into them.

Anyone who has lifted a Webster's Unabridged Dictionary knows his language is a weighty resource. If you have ever squeezed out a dozen mounds of delicious color onto a palette and then stood bemused, ruminating on the infinite possible combinations of color and value, you can't help being impressed by the comforts of limit. Stricture and structure go to the very core of things. To walk without a skeleton would be difficult, and a dance without one might have more sprawl than style. From my studio I often see a sailboat heeling, but never heeling without sails. Only resistance can reveal the shape of the wind and its strength.

It's as difficult to write clearly and simply as it is to make a drawing which sums up your reaction to a visual experience in the fewest and most telling lines. The difference between good and indifferent drawing is gossamer. The same can be said of writing. It is on just those frail threads the crucial differences hang. In both media clarity is dangerous, for it lays bare the quality of your thought and feeling for all to see; the cryptic is much safer. Nothing, artfully obscured, may just possibly be something. Given care and choice there are few subtleties or nuances outside the range of the scrupulous craftman. It is the artist's minimum obligation to know what he means and to convey that meaning to others. People who go around talking to themselves aren't always sane, and they are usually poor company.

When I first came to the island I made the acquaintance of an old man who, in his youth, had shipped aboard a square-rigger. As he told me his tales of storm and peril, the figure of a seaman reefing sail in a welter of wind seemed in some ways suggestive of the artist. The sailor must wrestle with the stubborn materials of the sails and at the same time keep his toe-hold on the thin guy-lines which are all there is between him and eternity. The thin line of direction and theme must sustain the artist amidst a chaos of choices. We do not ask that the storm harassed sailor wage his struggle with nonchalance. It is otherwise with the artist. We ask that his performance or his product has a jaunty air. We prefer lilt to labor. I might add that whenever I listened to this venerable survivor another important distinction came to mind. The sailor who loses his toe-hold is likely to pay the ultimate price. The artist can try again.

The native doubleness of the arts is the artist's delight and dilemma. Some apparently specific idea or experience spurs him to work. At the outset this initial impulse seems clear and exciting. It has a deceptive air of simplicity. Yet in the working, the specific may turn out to have been but a vague intimation. In the shaping it is likely to become intractable and baffling. It comes to have a will of its own. It is a kind of affirmation of something which didn't really exist before it was affirmed. Having assumed its final shape, it then seems predestined, and there are even times when the artist feels himself to be as much spectator as participant.

It does not follow, however, that the artist can set out on his voyage of discovery without checking his "beautiful peagreen boat" for leaks and sprung caulking. His frail craft may take him to an unanticipated harbor, but if it isn't held together with some ribbings of meaning and purpose it will fail to arrive at any harbor. It will founder on the cross-chop of infinite choice. Its pieces will end up as a litter of inconsequence on the beaches of self-indulgence.

Art, indeed, must mean what it says. To be memorable, it must say more than it means. If an art is wholly rational the observer yawns; if it is unremittingly irrational the spectator is like a man trying to keep his footing on buttered ice. The excitement lies in the reconciliation of incompatibles. On some few, rare, wonderful occasions the artist can induce the lion of eternity to lie down with the lamb of time.

Art may be but the form feeling takes. It must be not static form, but form plus pulse, and it must include some waywardness as an ingredient lest it petrify into formula. Sometimes when I've gone out in a boat the dolphins, or *puffers* as they're called on the island, have discovered it. From nowhere they are there. With circus abandon they cavort, putting on the full show as much for themselves as for us. Antic and agile, it's the sheer joy of it they're after. The glistening, dark blue shapes cleave the surface of the dark blue sea in a gesture of the utmost grace and, the arc fulfilled, disappear beneath the surface. When he succeeds, the artist arrests this momentary vision in order to feel his way into it in the hope that he may shape and share his feeling. In so doing, he must at all costs avoid the twin traps of dogma and doctrine. He is out to capture his quarry alive.

For its audience, the arts should simultaneously provide an answer and deepen a mystery. They should persuade us to know something in our heart through the language of common astonishment and should persist in the memory as the pungence of smoke clings the day after we have burnt over a blueberry patch.

Those who work in the arts seem to have no difficulty turning their biases into gospel. Perhaps this is inevitable; a totally bland tolerance is insipid, some friction is a part of energy. It may be that the artist shares the common human prejudice that to define something is to understand it, to name it is to know it. Of all people he should know better. We are told that "in the beginning was the Word." Before there could be the "word" something had to appear in the void to which the word or the name could be applied. Anything of ultimate consequence is indefinable. I can state with confidence I do not know what art is. Neither does anyone else. Say it's one thing and watch it appear in another guise; it will not stay put for measurement. Realizing it's an evasive target I've loosed some shots at the bullseye in the hope that some near misses might provide a clue to its location.

One last speculation: it may be that an island is a living metaphor for art itself; its known restrictions like the chosen enclosures of a print or a verse. But with all those connotations of unity and variety that notion seems too highflown. It isn't suggestive enough of tidal transformations. It's too vague to make us feel the caprice of weather in the order of the seasons, each with its floral signature; the rank vigor of field daisies; the furled flags of swamp iris buds; the thorned fragility of wild roses; the dauntless melancholy of the final aster (*frost flowers* they are called on the island); to the ultimate flowers of frost which are flakes of snow. It's too elevated to include the tart and sometimes testy humors of the island people and their sharp wisdoms. You don't hear in it the sounding presence of the sea. It leaves out something downright and daily, without which we are left only the thin gruel of idea and the parched consolations of aesthetics. The austere enchantments of a Maine island are its own closely guarded secrets. It is perhaps better that this should be so. To praise may be better than to pry.

One fore-noon I was down at the shore talking to an old lobsterman. His face was tanned and gaunt and scored with the marks of survival. His eyes were as startlingly blue as two drops of sea water. As he worked, his hands seemed to do the job from memory; a quick peck at the bristle of trap-nails in his mouth, a sure jab of the nail into the lath, and one true stroke of the hammer. No haste and no misses. His talk, as it filtered through the oral porcupine, was punctuated by the sound of the hammer. We discussed his calling and the weather in about equal parts. It was a fine day. The light and the lay of the land made the hills of Mt.

Desert as mountainy as they ever get. The islands stretched out in the light. The sea broke up the light and sent it caroming back toward the sun.

I said to the lobsterman, "What a beautiful view." It wasn't anything very striking to say about the view. It said it much better about itself.

He glanced up from his work and gave the hills, the islands, and the sea a careful, cataloging look. "Well," he replied, "They're real sightly...but you can't eat 'em." He paused and added, "I wouldn't want to do without 'em."

Neither would I.

A PUBLISHER'S NOTE

VIEWS FROM THE ISLAND was originally published by David Godine of Boston, in an edition of 110. This extreme limitation was dictated not by a calculated cultivation of rarity, but by the printing difficulties of the hand-done collagraph-intaglios which accompanied the poems. Most copies of that first version ended up in the rare-book collections of universities and bibliophiles. Satisfactory as those tangible tributes to the book's quality were, there was also a lingering sense that a wider currency would afford wider pleasure. In this revised version some of the original 30 sonnets have been altered or re-written. Thirty-two sonnets written since the first publication have been added. Eight of the original prints and one new print have been scrupulously reproduced by photo-offset, a medium better suited to contemporary book production and economics. The Tidal Press is, and will remain, a publisher of modest sized editions, but the publication of a modest sized edition rather than a minuscule edition makes VIEWS FROM THE ISLAND available to a wider audience.

A NOTE ON THE AUTHOR

CHARLES E. WADSWORTH, a painter and print-maker, who has shown widely in both group and one-man shows, is represented in a number of museums and private collections. His prints have appeared in "ROOT AND SKY", a selection of poetry from the plays of Christopher Fry; "SEED LEAVES", a poem of Richard Wilbur's, in homage to Robert Frost; "THE LONG SOUGHT LANDSCAPE", a memorial collection of poems by Charles Seymour Alden; and "ISLANDS OFF MAINE", by the Welsh poet, Leslie Norris.

1250
copies of Views
From   The   Island,
designed by James Fleming
and Charles E. Wadsworth have
been printed by The Furbush-Roberts
Press on Mohawk Superfine in a typeface called
Baskerville. The 1200 copies of the trade-
edition have been bound by The
Craftsmen Book-Binders.
50 de-luxe copies,
bound
in
quarter
leather with
marbled   boards   by
Gray Parrot have been
numbered and signed by
the author and artist,
Charles E. Wadsworth.